THE
UGLY
TRUTH

When Our Thoughts
Become Our Worst Enemy

VOLUME 1

THE WAR IN MY MIND

TABLE OF CONTENTS

NOTE TO
THE READER

This book is about saying the things we all think from time to time—but are often too afraid to say out loud.

Afraid of being judged.
Afraid of being misunderstood.
Afraid of being exposed. Afraid of being left out.

But here's what I've learned: I don't need anyone's permission to speak my truth, share my testimony, or drop a GPS pin to show exactly where I am on this journey toward becoming the best version of myself.

You'll find moments of honesty in these pages that may feel familiar—because silent struggles don't discriminate. My hope is that by reading mine, you feel empowered to confront yours.

I didn't write this book because I have it all together. I wrote it because I know what it feels like to fall apart—and not tell a soul.

There was a time when I couldn't sleep. Couldn't focus. Couldn't pray past my anxiety. I smiled, laughed, and showed up for everyone while silently falling apart inside. And the worst part? I thought I was alone.

But I'm not. And neither are you.

So, if your mind has ever been your battlefield... welcome.

If you've ever looked in the mirror and barely recognized yourself... this is for you.

If you've ever begged God to quiet the noise in your head... you're not going crazy—and you're not weak.

You're in a spiritual war and the battlefield is your mind.

You don't have to carry shame for what you thought. You don't have to live bound to what someone else spoke over you. And you don't have to walk through this healing alone.

This book is a mirror and a tool. A flashlight and a sword.

Use it. Mark it up. Cry on these pages if you have to – But whatever you do, don't allow your thoughts to keep you hostage and never give up.

Because the same God who created your mind is the One who knows how to bring it peace.

Let's begin.

With Love,
Kelly

INTRODUCTION

◆ I Was Good Until ◆
I Wasn't

Let's be clear—I didn't always feel broken. In fact, for most of my life, I felt good about myself. I walked in rooms like I belonged there. I smiled in the mirror with confidence - I knew I was smart, bold, worthy, and beautiful.

But then life happened.

And not the cute, filtered version of life either. I'm talking about betrayal. Shame. Being overlooked. People loving me wrong—or not at all. Carrying everybody else's weight while silently drowning in my own. And little by little, the version of me I once loved started to disappear.

The ugliest truth we can ever face…

IS THE ONE WE REFUSE
TO FACE ABOUT OURSELVES.

Now - That's the ugly truth.

Some days I questioned my worth. Some days I smiled through the pain. And other days, I just didn't feel like showing up at all.

But even in the chaos, God kept showing up.

He reminded me of who I was through little things—and sometimes through people. Almost 20 years ago, He sent me someone. Not perfect. Not polished. But God-fearing and full of potential. I'm glad I didn't just look at his current circumstances—I looked at his heart. And we grew together. It wasn't always easy. There was a lot of forgiving. Not judging. Praying. Starting over. But we held on.

And let me be honest—having someone amazing doesn't fix what's still broken inside. You can be loved deeply and still feel alone if you haven't healed the parts of yourself that don't believe you deserve it. That's not on them. That's on you. I had to face the me inside of me—the one battling self-doubt, fear, unworthiness, and shame. Because no amount of love from someone else can override the lies you keep repeating to yourself.

So no, this isn't a story about pity. This is about truth and triumph. It's for the ones who've been strong too long. Who look fine but feel forgotten. Who pour into everyone else and feel empty at the end of the day.

◆

I wrote this for you and the writing became therapy for me.

To remind you of who you are.

To remind you that you're not alone.

To remind you that even in the mess—especially in the mess— God still sees beauty.

And if you forgot how powerful you really are, don't worry.

We're about to remember together.

◆

· Section 1 ·

THE WAR IN MY MIND

Opening

Somewhere along the way, those outside voices became our own inner voices – louder, meaner, and harder to ignore. That's how it works: the enemy plants the seed, but we water it with our own thoughts.

We become our own worst critics. Our own worst enemies.

And when that happens, we start rehearsing everything that went wrong—who hurt us, who left, what failed—and we sit in it so long that it starts to define us. We focus on what we can't control and neglect the one thing we can: healing.

Listen to me: we've got to stop waiting on people to fix what they never broke. And if they did break it? It's still our job to put ourselves back together. But not alone. Prayer changes everything.

You were never meant to stay broken. You were never meant to live in that headspace of fear, doubt, and shame. This chapter is your moment to call out the lies, challenge your thoughts, and take back your peace. Because the war may be in your mind—but the victory is in your spirit.

Life has a slick way of becoming your narrator. It whispers things to you when you're at your weakest and dares you to believe them. It tells you you're ugly because someone didn't choose you. That you're too broken because something happened to you. That you're not enough—because you're not her, not him, not them. And sometimes, the people who should've protected you are the very ones who plant those lies deepest.

> **"It didn't matter how strong I was on the outside. Those words started to sound like facts. Until one day, I realized: *just because it was said doesn't mean it's true.*"**

THE UGLY TRUTH WE OVERLOOK ABOUT OURSELVES

Let's be honest.

We've mastered the art of deflection, denial, and disguise. But until we face the truths we'd rather ignore, we'll stay stuck in cycles that quietly destroy us.

You may not admit it, but most of us are secretly addicted to approval. We post for likes. We move for applause. We pretend not to care, but deep down we crave the claps.

 The Ugly Truth: If we're not careful, our self-worth will keep swinging on the hinges of other people's validation.

We want change—but we stay the same. We complain more than we act.

 The Ugly Truth: Complaining is comfortable. Consistency is a challenge that can feel like a chore.

What we criticize in others often reflects what we hate or fear in ourselves. Honestly, we project our own pain.

 The Ugly Truth: Their freedom offends us because it mirrors the chains we're still wearing.

We really are not ready to heal yet. It means stepping outside of our comfort zone. We say we're tired of the pain but keep inviting it over for dinner.

 The Ugly Truth: Healing means accountability, and that's harder than heartbreak.

We sabotage our own peace. Just when joy shows up, we pick a fight with it.

 The Ugly Truth: We've convinced ourselves that struggle is our default setting.

We must stop being emotionally lazy. We want people to just "meet us where we are at" without doing the work of communication.

 The Ugly Truth: It's easier to blame others for not understanding us than to meet them half way which requires effort.

We speak faith but move in fear. We trust our own trauma more than God.

 The Ugly Truth: We say "God got me" but live like trauma is the real savior.

We want forgiveness for ourselves but crucify others for their mistakes. We want grace but refuse to give it to others.

 The Ugly Truth: We demand for ourselves what we're unwilling to extend to others.

Productivity is our drug. We fear stillness because it forces us to face the parts of us that are still bleeding. We stay busy to avoid others.

 The Ugly Truth: Sometimes "I'm busy" is just code for "I'm broken."

We scroll and scroll… and wish silently. Secretly comparing ourselves to others and coveting what they have.

 The Ugly Truth: What we call "admiration" is often dressed-up envy.

It's not easy facing the truth.

But here's what I know:

God can't heal who you're pretending to be.

He can only restore the version of you who shows up raw, real, and ready.

THE COMPANY YOU KEEP & THE CONTENT YOU CONSUME

Your mind is a sponge.

It absorbs more than you realize—conversations, environments, music, TV shows, social media posts, podcasts, and the attitudes of those closest to you. Every interaction has an effect. Every voice becomes part of the background noise that shapes how you see yourself and the world around you.

SO HERE'S A TRUTH WE DON'T SAY ENOUGH:

Who you spend time with matters.

What you listen to matters.

What you read and meditate on matters.

If you surround yourself with chaos, negativity, or people who don't challenge you to grow—your mind will mirror that. It will get stuck in survival mode, constantly reacting instead of healing.

On the flip side, when you're intentional with your surroundings—peace becomes more accessible. You begin to recognize the weight that certain people, spaces, and habits place on your mental well-being.

Your mind needs exercise, just like your body. It needs rest, renewal, and positive reinforcement. And that means intentionally feeding it things that help—not harm.

Here's what that can look like:

- Repeating affirmations—even when you don't fully believe them yet.
- Speaking life over yourself when no one else does.
- Meditating on scriptures that ground you and give you strength.

- Doing a puzzle or reading a book that stimulates your imagination.

- Journaling the things you're grateful for.

- Listening to jazz, worship, or silence—whatever calms your soul.

- Taking breaks from people, screens, and places that drain you.

You don't need to wait until you're at your breaking point to take care of your mind. Prevention is just as important as healing.

So guard your mind. Nourish your soul. Set boundaries.

And don't be afraid to walk away from anything that threatens your peace.

You deserve to live free—and that starts by choosing what and who has access to your mental space.

Interactive Journal

THE COMPANY YOU KEEP & THE CONTENT YOU CONSUME

Reflection Prompt

Think about the people you spend the most time with and the content you consume daily (social media, TV, music, books). How do they shape your thoughts, words, and actions?

_____

_____

_____

_____

_____

SELF-CHECK

Circle which ones apply to you most often:

☐ I spend time with people who drain me instead of build me.

☐ I often compare myself to what I see on social media.

☐ I watch or listen to content that doesn't align with my values.

☐ I rarely evaluate whether my influences are positive or negative.

☐ I struggle to disconnect from content that distracts me from my goals.

Affirmation
Prayer Space

Affirmation to Write & Repeat:

"I will choose company and content that speak life, truth, and growth into me."

Rewrite it several times below:

_____

_____

_____

_____

_____

_____

Action Step

What one change will you make this week in the company you keep or the content you consume?

_____

_____

_____

_____

Interactive Journal
THE CHOICES WE REGRET

Reflection Prompt

What are the loudest thoughts that replay in your mind daily? Write down at least three of them.

_____

_____

_____

_____

_____

_____

_____

SELF-CHECK

Circle which ones apply to you most often:

☐ I replay past choices and feel stuck in regret.

☐ I struggle to forgive myself for mistakes I've made.

☐ I hide parts of my story because I feel ashamed.

☐ I let past regrets keep me from making new decisions.

☐ I rarely see the growth that came from my mistakes.

AFFIRMATION
Prayer Space

AFFIRMATION TO WRITE & REPEAT:

"My past choices do not define me.
God redeems my mistakes and uses
them for my growth."

REWRITE IT SEVERAL TIMES BELOW:

_____

_____

_____

_____

_____

_____

ACTION STEP

What is one regret you are ready to release today, and what truth will you replace it with?

_____

_____

_____

_____

TURNING POINT
From Mental Trap to Mindful Healing

At some point, I had to stop and ask myself: How much of my pain is self-inflicted? Not because I caused the original wound—but because I kept reopening it with my thoughts.

The turning point wasn't loud or dramatic. It was subtle—a shift in awareness. I realized the battle wasn't just with what happened to me; it was with what I kept telling myself about what happened to me.

That's when everything changed.

I saw that the same mind that had rehearsed pain could also rehearse peace. The same thoughts that had kept me stuck could be retrained to set me free.

BUT IT HAD TO START WITH ME MAKING A DECISION:

No more feeding the lies.

No more marinating in the mess.

No more waiting for someone else
to heal what they didn't hurt.

It wasn't instant. Growth rarely is.

But it began with small steps:

Challenging the lies I'd adopted as truth.

Replacing shame with grace.

Repeating God's promises until they drowned out the enemy's whispers.

Creating space—mentally, emotionally, and physically—for healing to land.

It wasn't about pretending everything was okay. It was about refusing to let everything that wasn't okay define me anymore.

That's when the war in my mind began to shift.

Not because life stopped being hard, but because I stopped letting it break me in the same places.

And for the first time in a long time—I started to see myself clearly again.

Not as a victim. Not as a mistake. Not as someone barely surviving.

But as someone fighting back.

As someone healing forward.

As someone finally free enough to choose peace over the pit.

This chapter exposes the lies life tries to convince us of—through trauma, rejection, silence, abuse, or even just the quiet battles of everyday struggle. But it doesn't stop there.

Somewhere along the way, those outside voices became my own inner voice—and let me tell you, it was louder than anything anyone else ever said. That's how it works: the enemy plants the seed, but we water it with our thoughts.

I became my own worst enemy.

I replayed old pain like it was on loop. I second-guessed my worth. I stared in mirrors and didn't see the same woman anymore—not because of what people did, but because of what I believed.

We do this.

We keep our focus on things that steal our joy and rob our peace.

No more.

The moment I stopped waiting on apologies and started taking ownership of my healing, everything shifted. Not overnight—but over time. And not alone—with God.

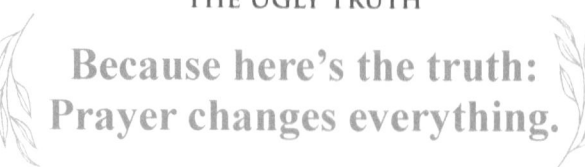

Because here's the truth:
Prayer changes everything.

It's not just a spiritual practice—it's a strategy. A lifeline. A way to fight back when your thoughts try to take you under.

Let this chapter be a mirror, not a magnifying glass.

Don't use it to judge others—use it to examine yourself.

REFLECTION PROMPT

What thoughts have been silently waging war in your mind?

Write them down without judgment. Be honest. Be raw.

Then challenge each one—cross out the lie and write the truth beneath it.

ASK YOURSELF:

Where did this thought come from?

Who told me this, and why did I believe it?

What does God say about me instead?

This is where the healing begins—when truth finally speaks louder than your wounds.

What lie are you still living with that someone else planted but you've been repeating to yourself?

Write it down. Then cross it out.

Now rewrite your OWN truth.

TRUTH BOMBS

- Just because I think it doesn't make it true.

- I am not the voice in my head on my worst day.

- Healing begins when I stop rehearsing pain.

- My mind is powerful—but I have the authority to redirect it.

- I don't have to accept every thought that knocks on my door.

- God's truth is louder than my trauma.

- If I wouldn't say it to someone I love, I won't say it to myself.

- What I feed my mind will either free me or finish me – make a choice.

- Peace is possible—even here.

AFFIRMATIONS

I take back my thoughts.

I cast down every lie.

I no longer agree with fear, shame, or self-doubt.

My past does not define me.

My mistakes do not disqualify me.

My mind may be a battlefield, but I no longer fight alone.

My value is not up for debate.

I speak life over myself—even when no one else does.

I release what broke me and receive what's healing me.

God's Word anchors me when my thoughts try to drift.

I am not the voices of my trauma.

I am not what they said.

I am not stuck—I am evolving.

My mind is being renewed.

Peace is my portion.

Healing is my birthright.

And I declare—my mind is under new management.

PERSONAL TESTIMONIAL

I remember walking across the stage after earning my second master's degree—something most people never even dream of. But instead of feeling victorious, the first thought that hit me was:

"I should've lost 20 pounds."

Really? I had just accomplished something extraordinary. I looked beautiful. I had overcome the odds, sacrificed, studied, and pushed through. And yet... I let my joy be hijacked by a number on a scale.

That thought passed. Thank God.

But then another one came.

"You've got all these degrees, and you're still not getting paid your worth."

Here I was, doing everything "right"—educating myself, applying, interviewing—and still watching doors close. I started wondering, What do they see when they look at me? I used to command rooms, get hired on the spot. Now I'm being told "you're amazing" in interviews and still not getting the job.

It didn't stop there. In the course of one day, my mind went on a whole journey:

- My parents' divorce
- My dad remarrying
- My husband looking at another woman

- Friends who betrayed me

- Wishing I had a sister

- Missing my grandmother

And a deep, aching need to just feel safe in a world that feels like it's on fire.

I honestly felt like I was this close to a full-blown breakdown. And then I remembered something tragic:

I was out of PTO. ☹

That moment of humor saved me. Because I had to check myself, real quick. Sometimes, I have to talk to myself like I'm 7 years old:

"Girl... if you don't wipe your eyes and get back to reality, you're about to have real problems. Right now your problems are in your head—but if you don't stop, they're going to be on your back, pushing you into a wall."

That's when I realized the ugliest truth:

My thoughts were doing more damage than life ever did.

And that's what this chapter is about. Not just the lies that came from the outside... but the ones we recycled inside.

Interactive Journal

THE WAR IN MY MIND

These prompts are designed to help you process the lies, reflect on your truth, and reframe your thoughts with the Word of God.

1. Identify the Lie

What is one negative thought or lie that continues to play on repeat in your mind?

2. Who Planted That Lie?

Where do you think that lie originated? Was it a person, a moment, or a past experience?

3. Rewrite the Truth

What truth can you speak over that lie today? What would God say about you instead?

4. Your Mirror Talk

If you looked in the mirror today and talked to yourself like someone you love, what would you say?

5. Faith Over Feelings

Name one area of your life where you need to choose faith over feelings. What scripture or truth are you going to stand on?

6. Declare Your Truth

Write a declaration over your mind. Example: "Today, I take every thought captive. I am not who my past says I am. I am who God says I am."

REFLECTION PROMPT

What are the loudest thoughts that replay in your mind daily? Write down at least three of them.

_____

_____

_____

_____

_____

_____

_____

_____

_____

_____

_____

_____

_____

_____

SELF-CHECK

Circle which ones apply to you most often:

☐ I replay mistakes from the past.

☐ I assume the worst before it happens.

☐ I tell myself I'm not good enough.

☐ I compare myself to others.

☐ I procrastinate out of fear.

AFFIRMATION
Prayer Space

AFFIRMATION TO WRITE & REPEAT:

"My mind is not my enemy.
God has given me power, love,
and a sound mind."

REWRITE IT SEVERAL TIMES BELOW:

_____

_____

_____

_____

_____

_____

_____

_____

ACTION STEP

What's one thought you will replace with truth this week? Write it here:

_____

_____

_____

_____

_____

· Section 2 ·

THE MASK I WORE

Opening

We all wear masks.

Some of us wear them so well, we forget what our real faces even look like. Not because we're fake—but because we've been forced to function while wounded. Life didn't wait for us to heal, so we learned how to hide.

Some masks look like confidence. Others look like being the strong friend. Humor. Hustle. Some of us wear a smile to hide sadness. Others wear control to hide fear. And some of us—if we're honest—have worn strength so long we wouldn't know what vulnerability felt like if it introduced itself.

That's the thing about masks—they're not always malicious. Sometimes they're survival. We wear them to avoid judgment. To avoid shame. To avoid breakdowns that might happen if we ever stopped performing. We wear them because life didn't give us safe places to fall apart.

Serving everybody else until we're empty. For some, the mask is being the fixer, the overachiever, the peacemaker. For others, it's control—because the chaos we survived taught us we couldn't afford to let go.

And what's wild? We became so good at it, even we forgot we were wearing a mask.

But the truth is—what you hide, can't heal.

Wearing a mask may protect your reputation, your image, or even your relationships. But it also blocks restoration. It keeps God's grace from reaching the places you refuse to expose. Because God can't bless who you pretend to be. He can only heal the real you.

Let's stop equating vulnerability with weakness.

Let's stop calling emotional shutdown "being private" when it's really a trauma response.

Because hiding might feel safe—but healing requires honesty.

BUT THE TRUTH IS:

Masks may protect you, but they also prevent you from healing. Because God can't bless who you pretend to be. He can only heal the real you.

Let's tell the truth.

We don't just wear makeup, clothes, or designer fits. We wear invisible masks—crafted from fear, shame, trauma, and silence.

We smile when we're sad.

We cheer others on while secretly crumbling inside.

We play strong because "falling apart" feels like failure.

 The Ugly Truth: We'd rather look blessed than admit we feel broken.

And for some of us, the mask is control.

We try to orchestrate how we're perceived, what people say, and how situations unfold—all because letting go feels too vulnerable.

 The Ugly Truth: Controlling everything is just another mask we wear to hide how scared we really are.

We avoid silence because it reminds us of what still hurts.

We avoid stillness because it exposes what we're still carrying.

So we scroll, shop, plan, overcommit, and perform.

 The Ugly Truth: "Staying busy" often means we're staying distracted from the real healing we need.

We're embarrassed by where we come from.

We feel unworthy because of our childhood.

We carry guilt for family members, spouses, and children whose actions make us question our identity.

 The Ugly Truth: We let shame become the narrator of our story— when it was never meant to have a mic.

AND HERE'S ANOTHER ONE:
We fear that if people knew the real us, they'd walk away.

So we keep filtering. Keep faking. Keep adjusting ourselves to fit rooms that aren't even meant for us.

 The Ugly Truth: The people who won't love the real you can't love the fake version either.

At the root of it all, we think image will save us.

We believe if we look good enough, successful enough, strong enough… we'll be enough.

BUT HERE'S THE PART WE DON'T SAY OUT LOUD:

No outfit, no degree, no house, no vacation, no car, no follower count, no church position, and no savings account can satisfy a soul that's tired of pretending.

 The Ugly Truth: Until we take the mask off, we'll keep gasping for air beneath the weight of our own performance.

It's time to come up for air.

It's time to stop protecting the fake version of you and start healing the real one.

Because God can't bless the mask.

He can only bless the raw, honest, broken version of you that shows up anyway.

THE REAL REASON WE WEAR MASKS

Let's be real—it's not always about protecting ourselves from others. Sometimes, the mask is protection from ourselves.

We wear masks to hide the truth we haven't made peace with.

The childhood we'd rather forget.

The Choices We Regret.

The shame we carry from broken families, toxic relationships, addictions, or the burden of someone else's decisions.

We wear masks to avoid judgment—but deep down, we fear exposure more than rejection.

We tell ourselves, "If they knew the real me… they'd walk away."

So instead, we give them a curated version: polite, polished, and safe.

BUT HERE'S THE HARD TRUTH:

*The people who can't love the real,
raw, redeemed version of you… won't love
the fake, filtered version either.*

So why not show up as your whole self?

We only get one life. One.

And this isn't a dress rehearsal. There are no do-overs—just decisions.

You don't have to prove your worth through performance.

You don't have to keep pretending you're okay when you're unraveling inside.

You don't have to shrink, edit, or apologize for being a work in progress.

Because God doesn't heal the person you pretend to be—He heals the one brave enough to be honest.

**What we really need is time
in God's presence.
In His Word.
In truth.**

In community with people who love us, not despite our wounds—but because we've survived them.

Your spirit is tired because it's begging to be seen.

Begging to stop performing.
Begging to heal.
So take the mask off.
Let the healing begin with the real you.

TURNING POINT
When the Mask Begins to Slip

Pretending works... until it doesn't.

Eventually, the weight of your mask gets too heavy. You start forgetting where the performance ends and your real self begins. You laugh, but it's hollow. You show up, but you're drained. You help others, but no one sees you drowning.

I know that feeling. I've lived in it.

You say "I'm fine" so often it becomes your script—even when your soul is screaming for help. You carry everyone else's burdens because it's easier than sitting with your own. And even though people praise your strength, inside you're asking, "But who carries me?"

Here's the wake-up call: the mask may have worked for a season, but it cannot sustain your breakthrough.

There comes a moment when you either peel it off—or it falls off during your collapse.

When I let God start removing my mask, I was terrified—but I was also free. Free from pretending. Free from performing. Free from the pressure of being "okay" when I wasn't. And in that freedom, I found the me I forgot existed.

Not the perfect version.

Not the polished, put-together one.

The real one.

And she was worthy all along.

REFLECTION PROMPT

* What mask have you been wearing out of survival?

* What would it look like to finally lay it down?

* Write it out. Then ask yourself—who would I be if I allowed God to heal the version of me I've been hiding?

* What kind of mask have you worn to get through life? Who did you feel you had to be?

TRUTH BOMBS

My mask helped me survive, but it won't help me heal.

Pretending to be okay is not the same as being okay.

Hiding my wounds doesn't make them disappear—it makes them fester.

I don't have to perform for love. I was worthy before I proved anything.

God can handle the real me—and that's who He wants.

* Pretending protects pain—it doesn't heal it.

* If vulnerability scares you, healing will stretch you.

* God can't bless the version of you that's not real.

* Wearing a mask might keep people comfortable—but it keeps you confined.

WORKBOOK ACTIVITY
"Me vs. My Mask"

What My Mask Looks Like: _____

What I'm Hiding Beneath It: _____

What God Says About the Real Me: _____

"Who Am I Without the Mask?"

Add your own below...

_____
_____
_____
_____
_____
_____
_____
_____
_____
_____
_____
_____
_____
_____
_____
_____
_____
_____
_____

AFFIRMATION
"I'm Worth Showing Up As Me"

I no longer need to wear what doesn't fit.

I release the mask.

I don't have to perform, pretend, or prove.

I am loved—even in my rawest form.

I am seen—even when I don't smile.

I am safe to take off the mask—because healing lives in honesty.

"I no longer hide behind strength—I rise in authenticity."

"I realize healing can't reach what I hide."

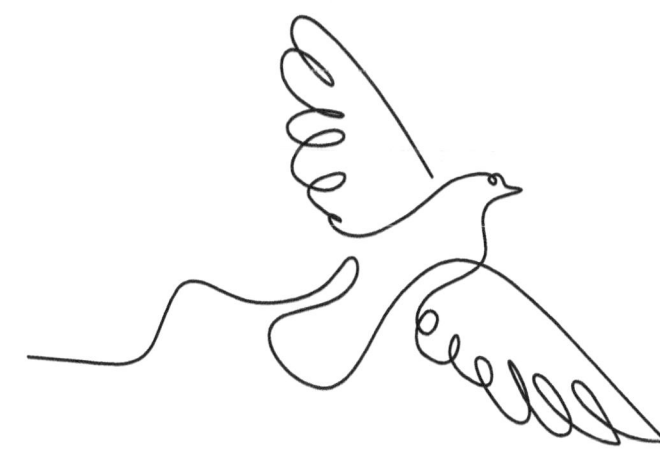

Interactive Journal

THE UGLY TRUTH WE OVERLOOK ABOUT OURSELVES

Reflection Prompt

What's one truth about yourself you often avoid facing?

_____

_____

_____

_____

_____

_____

_____

SELF-CHECK

Circle which ones apply to you most often:

☐ I minimize my own pain and act like I'm fine.

☐ I put others first so much that I lose myself.

☐ I downplay my accomplishments and worth.

☐ I avoid silence because I don't want to face my thoughts.

☐ I pretend I've forgiven, but deep down I haven't.

AFFIRMATION
Prayer Space

AFFIRMATION TO WRITE & REPEAT:

"I am not defined by the truths
I've ignored. I am defined by
the truth God speaks over me."

REWRITE IT SEVERAL TIMES BELOW:

ACTION STEP

What is one overlooked truth about yourself that you are willing to face today?

WHO AM I WITHOUT THE MASK
Who Do I Pretend to Be

Reflection Prompt

Think about the 'mask' you wear around others. Who do you pretend to be, and what parts of your true self stay hidden?

_____

_____

_____

_____

_____

_____

_____

_____

_____

SELF-CHECK

Circle which ones apply to you most often:

- ☐ I act strong when I feel weak inside.
- ☐ I pretend to be happy while silently hurting.
- ☐ I hide my true opinions to avoid conflict.
- ☐ I downplay my gifts or talents to fit in.
- ☐ I wear different 'masks' depending on who I'm around.

AFFIRMATION
Prayer Space

AFFIRMATION TO WRITE & REPEAT:

"I am fearfully and wonderfully made.
I no longer need to hide behind a mask;
my true self is enough."

REWRITE IT SEVERAL TIMES BELOW:

_____

_____

_____

_____

_____

_____

_____

ACTION STEP

What mask are you ready to take off, and what truth about yourself will you walk in instead?

_____

_____

_____

_____

· Section 3 ·

SILENT STRUGGLES

Opening

Some struggles scream. Others whisper.

But the most dangerous ones? They stay silent.

Silent struggles don't show up in ER visits or prayer requests. They show up in cancelled plans, fake smiles, and long stares into nothing.

They sound like "I'm fine" when you're anything but.

WE'VE ALL BEEN THERE.

- Scrolling for hours to numb the pain.

- Keeping busy so we don't have to feel.

- Pouring into others because helping them hurts less than helping ourselves.

Just because someone looks okay doesn't mean they are.

And just because you're functioning doesn't mean you're healing.

THE MIND'S TRAP

The mind is powerful—but sometimes, it's not our protector. Sometimes, it becomes our prison.

It plays tricks on us, setting traps we don't even realize we're walking into. And instead of pausing to breathe, reflect, or dismantle the lie— we fall in. Headfirst. No questions asked.

Why?

Because the trap feels familiar. Comfortable, even.

See, pain has a strange way of becoming home when you've lived in it long enough. And self-pity? It doesn't demand growth. It doesn't require accountability. You can just sit in it—unbothered, unchallenged, and unchanged.

YOU CAN HOST A FULL-BLOWN MENTAL PITY PARTY AND START TO BELIEVE:

◆ "This is just how life is."

◆ "Maybe I deserve this."

◆ "It's always been this way, so what's the point?"

The longer you sit there, the easier it is to let your wounds speak louder than your worth.

I know that trap well.

Overthinking and self-doubt used to feel like my closest companions. They showed up even when no one else did. They whispered insecurities, exaggerated problems, and magnified every flaw.

I was raised to pray. My mother taught me to pause before speaking—to process my emotions through prayer and reflection. But depending on the situation, it felt more urgent to defend myself. To explain. To get the last word in. To change someone's perception about who I really was.

But what I've learned is this: most of our mental battles don't come from others—they come from the war we create inside ourselves.

THEY'RE BUILT ON QUESTIONS WE NEVER ANSWER:

◆ What should I be doing by now?

◆ Why am I not further along?

◆ Why did this happen to me?

◆ Why hasn't it happened for me?

What you meditate on will eventually manifest. Your body, your energy, your decisions—they all follow your thoughts. The mind literally has the power to lead you to your demise—or your destiny.

It's that serious.

That's why we have to be intentional about what we allow in, what we repeat to ourselves, and how we fight back.

Because you can't win a battle you won't acknowledge.

And the war in your mind? It can be won—but not by pretending it doesn't exist.

 The Ugly Truth: We believe our thoughts because they sound like our voice—even when they're wrong.

We convince ourselves we're not qualified. Not lovable. Not capable. We talk ourselves out of blessings before they even reach our door.

 The Ugly Truth: Many of us reject ourselves before the world ever gets a chance to.

We assume people don't like us—when we really just don't like ourselves. We mislabel discernment as detachment and call it "guarding our peace" when it's really just avoidance rooted in fear.

 The Ugly Truth: Sometimes we don't want healing—we want hiding, because healing requires exposure.

We run from hard conversations. We minimize our own dreams. We compare. We scroll. We procrastinate. And then we wonder why we feel so empty, so lost, so disconnected from purpose.

 The Ugly Truth: Avoidance feels like protection, but it's really just a delay tactic dressed in comfort.

We can't think our way into peace while meditating on pain. The mind can only hold what we feed it. And some of us are starving spiritually because we've been feeding on negativity for far too long.

The Ugly Truth: You can't win a battle against the enemy when the enemy lives in your head rent-free.

And that's why the trap is so dangerous—because it's invisible. It's a cycle. A thought pattern. A quiet sabotage.

 The Ugly Truth: If you keep thinking the same, you'll keep living the same.

Your mind is either leading you toward breakthrough or breakdown. The choice isn't easy—but it's yours. Just because the thought shows up doesn't mean you have to sit with it, believe it, or let it shape your reality.

It's time to evict the lies.

It's time to renew your mind.

It's time to break the trap.

TURNING POINT
You are not your thoughts.

You have the power to challenge them, correct them, and replace them.

The Power of Naming It

The healing didn't start when I prayed harder. It didn't start when I talked to a friend.

IT STARTED WHEN I ADMITTED IT OUT LOUD: ***"I'm struggling."***

That one sentence broke the silence.

We think that speaking our truth makes us weak. But silence is what breaks us. When I finally gave language to my pain, I gave God permission to enter it.

REFLECTION PROMPT

* What are you silently carrying that no one knows about?

* What do you wish someone would ask you—but they never do?

TRUTH BOMBS

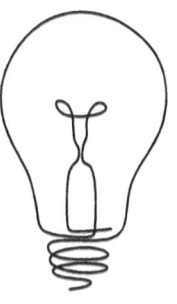

- Functioning doesn't mean healed.

- You can be surrounded and still feel unseen.

- Naming your struggle is the first step to ending it.

- God hears what you're afraid to say out loud.

AFFIRMATION

*"I no longer suffer in silence. My voice matters.
My healing matters."*

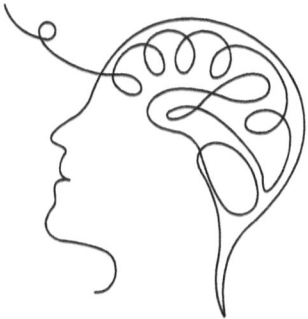

WORKBOOK ACTIVITY

Take a moment to reflect on the internal struggles you carry silently. Use the table below to identify what you've been holding in, why it remains hidden, and what healing could look like if you gave yourself permission to be honest.

"Unspoken But Felt"

COLUMN 1: The struggle I hide	COLUMN 2: Why I hide it	COLUMN 3: What healing might look like

REFLECTION

What thoughts do you need to release today? What truth do you need to hold onto instead?

· Section 4 ·

SHIFTING THE NARRATIVE

Rewrite Your Narrative

There comes a moment when you realize you've been living by a script you didn't even write...

MY OLD NARRATIVE:

_____

_____

_____

_____

_____

_____

_____

_____

MY NEW NARRATIVE:

_____

_____

_____

_____

_____

_____

_____

_____

STORYTELLING #1
Marriage Isn't for the Weak

Let's get one thing straight—
marriage is not for the weak.

And after being married three times (yes, three!), and now to the same amazing man for the past 20 years, I can say without hesitation:

I've learned a few things. And I've *unlearned* even more.

Marriage is beautiful, yes—but it's also humbling, stretching, and sanctifying.

What I didn't realize early on was just how much my identity—how I saw me—was wrapped up in how my husband treated me.

That's never a safe place to build your foundation.

Because when you tie your self-worth to someone else's actions, flaws, or attention span, their behavior becomes a mirror you start measuring yourself by. And that's dangerous.

I remember those early years. I remember feeling inadequate. I remember noticing his wandering eyes, and how deeply that cut—especially when I wasn't where I wanted to be in my own body or self-esteem.

He was looking… and I took that to mean I wasn't enough.

Disrespect, flirtation, dishonor—it all stung. But here's what I've learned since:

Had I been more invested in *Kelly*, it wouldn't have broken me the way it did.

Because when you carry yourself with confidence, when you invest in your growth, your peace, your joy…

You begin to walk in a way that commands respect—not in arrogance, but in quiet strength.

And when someone chooses not to honor that? It makes them look like a fool, not you.

It took a lot of prayer.

A lot of hard, honest conversations.

And a lot of choosing to *not give up* on each other—because we both grew. Together.

Now? We laugh about things that used to cause pain.

We communicate better.

And most importantly—we understand that loving someone doesn't mean losing yourself.

So to every woman reading this:
Never lose yourself for love.

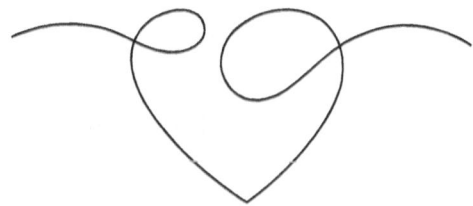

You are not a reflection of someone else's choices—you are a reflection of your own *healing* and *growth*.

If you're married, engaged, dating, or just trying to figure out your own heart…

Start by loving the woman in the mirror first.

Because if she's rooted, nobody—not even the person next to her—can shake her.

STORYTELLING #1
Marriage Isn't for the Weak (Part 2)

"Call 911...Because My Husband Isn't Coming!"

Marriage to someone who's been single for 42 years isn't exactly a walk in the park. My husband, **John Wilkerson**, is an incredible man—resilient, faithful, and transparent—but let me be honest: the transition from bachelor to husband was not smooth sailing. This man was used to coming and going as he pleased, dating whoever, whenever, with no one asking questions.

And then God sent *me*. ☺ His first wife... and I don't come with an instruction manual.

Now let me add this layer: John has been **clean for over 25 years** and is a recovering addict. His strength blows me away, and I've always tried to support him—even attending meetings and conferences. I remember the first time I went with him... I felt like I needed a shirt that said, *"Just here for moral support. Not recovering. Please don't pass me the mic."* ☺

Fast forward to a random night at 3:30 in the morning. Our phone rings.

John answers, and suddenly I hear him say:

> *"Oh my God... I'm on my way! Don't do anything. Just wait. Please wait. I'm coming!"*

He jumps up, throws on his pants, and starts rushing to the door.

I'm sitting there like... "Who is this woman calling my husband at 3:30 AM crying about a relapse?"

He says her name (we'll call her *Penny*), and explains she's about to relapse. I'm like, "Okay, give me the phone." He gives me this wide-eyed *What are you gonna say??* look. But I was calm. I had a plan.

I got on the phone, and I said:

> "Penny… girl… are you okay?"

She sobs, "No. I'm about to relapse. I can't do this."

> And I said, "Okay. I want you to hang up and call 911."

She paused: "Wait, what? Why would I call 911?"

> "Because John ain't coming over there today. So if you're about to relapse, get help—but you won't be getting it from my husband. Not tonight, sis."

And then I hung up the phone.

We laugh so hard about it now—and yes, Penny turned out just fine. But that moment showed both of us something real:

Love is powerful, but it needs boundaries.

And even in our most humorous moments, we were growing—learning to prioritize marriage, protect our peace, and support each other the *right* way.

Interactive Journal

GOD HONORS MARRIAGE AND SO SHOULD YOU
What Can You Do to Make It Work?

Reflection Prompt

Marriage is a covenant that God honors. Reflect on your role in your marriage (or future marriage). What can you do to strengthen it and show honor to God in the process?

_____

_____

_____

_____

_____

SELF-CHECK

Circle which ones you relate to most often:

- ☐ I sometimes take my spouse/partner for granted.
- ☐ I struggle to forgive quickly when I feel hurt.
- ☐ I prioritize work, friends, or hobbies over my relationship.
- ☐ I don't always communicate openly and honestly.
- ☐ I rarely pray with or for my spouse.

AFFIRMATION
Prayer Space

AFFIRMATION TO WRITE & REPEAT:

"I will honor marriage as God designed it, giving love, respect, and effort to make it thrive."

REWRITE IT SEVERAL TIMES BELOW:

_____

_____

_____

_____

_____

_____

_____

_____

_____

ACTION STEP

List three intentional actions you will take this week to strengthen your marriage or prepare yourself to be a godly spouse in the future:

_____

_____

_____

_____

THIS SECTION IS GIVING HONOR TO THE KIDS LEFT BEHIND

STORYTELLING #2
Don't Compromise Your Child's Innocence for Your Choices

I remember when I divorced my ex-husband and later married the love of my life—my husband John, who I'm still married to today. At that time, my daughter was just 11 years old. She had only ever known one man as her protector—her father, who had been a wonderful and present dad.

I was fiercely protective of her. I made a vow to myself that I would never parade men in and out of her life. No revolving door of boyfriends. No blurred boundaries. I refused to let my daughter carry the weight of my choices.

When John and I got married, I told him plainly:

> *"My daughter is loving by nature. You are not allowed to be alone with her. You're not allowed in her room. I trust you, but I will never know any man well enough to put him ahead of my daughter's safety."*

And I meant it.

When she was sick and I had to work, I didn't leave her home with him. Even though he worked the evening shift and was available during the day, I would take her to her grandparents or to her father. It wasn't about not loving my husband—it was about protecting my child at all costs.

Fast forward to today—my daughter is now 30 years old. She and John have an unbreakable bond, and she loves him deeply. And do you know what he told me?

He said,

> *"I respected you so much for how you protected your daughter. So many women I dated before you didn't even think twice about who their daughters were around. But you showed me what true motherhood looks like."*

And my daughter said,

> *"Mom, thank you for never compromising my innocence."*

To every woman who has walked through heartbreak, abandonment, or betrayal—please hear me:

Do not let your pain put your children in harm's way.

Do not compromise their innocence for your comfort, your loneliness, or your healing.

Stop leaving your children with men you barely know. And even if you think you know him, **keep both eyes open at all times**. It is your divine responsibility to protect your babies—spiritually, emotionally, and physically.

You can still fall in love. You can still heal.

But you don't have to sacrifice your child's safety in the process.

STORYTELLING #3
"You Look Nothing Like Beyonce"

Years ago, one of my boys—smart, vibrant, full of personality, ran into the house after school beaming with pride. He said,

> *"Mommy, I told everyone at school you look just like Oprah!"*

I laughed and asked, "Why Oprah? I'm feeling more Beyoncé today." He stared at me in deep silence… like he was *trying to figure out who I saw in the mirror*. Then he went outside and said nothing more.

A few days later, he got in trouble at school. The teacher called me. As always, that meant punishment—no phone, no TV. When he walked in, he was frustrated but composed.

> *"I know I'm on punishment," he said. "But since I'm already in trouble, I just wanna tell you—you don't look anything like Beyoncé. I only said that to make you feel good. You look nothing like Beyonce with your fat a**…"*

I hollered. I couldn't even be mad. He had clearly been going to bed for days hoping I wasn't *actually* serious about looking like Beyoncé. I still laugh about it to this day.

STORYTELLING #4
The Ones Who Stayed

There was another young man I had the privilege of loving—and to this day, he holds a special place in my heart.

He came to me carrying pain that no child should ever have to bear. He had been abused, neglected, and bounced around like he didn't matter. But he did matter. And he always will.

When he was finally able to reconnect with his biological family, I remember him being so excited to talk to them. But that joy quickly turned into heartbreak.

They found out he was living with a Black family—my husband and me—and their only response was:

*"You over there with those n*****s?"*

That word. That ugliness. That complete disregard for the love we had poured into him. I was angry—not for myself, but for him. For how broken you must be to throw hate at the very people who loved your child when you wouldn't... or couldn't.

But he rose above it.

Today, that same young man is thriving—successful, strong, and secure in who he is. He recently told my husband and me something that melted my heart completely. He said:

"Whenever I have kids, they're going to call you Grandma and Grandpa."

"Really?" I asked, *"You think so?"*

He smiled and said, "Absolutely. You earned that title."

He continued,

"My family knows now—I don't see color. Because the people they called horrible names are the same people who stayed. The ones who showed me love. The ones who fed me, clothed me, prayed over me, and gave me a home. Because of Kelly and John, I learned to see people for who they are... not what they look like."

That moment reminded me that love doesn't just heal—it teaches. It redefines what family looks like. It silences hate without ever raising its voice.

STORYTELLING #5
"Can You Promise No One Will Touch Me While I Sleep?"

Another boy came to live with me when he was only six. He had already been through more than most adults ever will. In one home, the foster parents let their biological kids put bugs in his bed—knowing full well he was terrified. They told him foster kids couldn't eat Pop-Tarts or real cereal. He was constantly reminded that he was *less than*.

When he came to my house, we welcomed him with cake and a party. He was confused at first, but we made sure he felt seen. That first night, I read to him and left a nightlight on. By 1 a.m., every light in the house was on. I turned them off and kissed his forehead. An hour later—*all the lights were back on.*

I walked into his room and gently asked, "Baby, what's wrong?" He looked at me with trembling eyes and said,

"Do you promise that while I'm asleep, you won't touch me?"

My heart shattered.

"I promise," I said. *"And I will protect you with my life."*

And I did.

That was over two decades ago, and that same boy is now a grown man. He still calls me mom, and the one thing he's never forgotten is that I *protected* him.

STORYTELLING #6
"You Can't Take Him!"

Another story still shakes me.

I had just returned from a cruise and was picking up one of my boys from a respite provider—another foster family who watches children while you're away. As soon as I pulled up, one boy—my son—ran out of the house and jumped into my car. I could see the dried tears on his face.

"I'll be right back," I told him. "I just need to grab your things."

When I walked in, I found another young boy crying so hard it looked like he had a nosebleed. I asked what happened.

"They let their younger siblings beat me up at the park," he sobbed.

My son in the car, still trembling, said,

"I didn't help him... I was scared I'd get beat up too."

The foster parents were barely in their 20s, and when I confronted them, they seemed clueless about why this was a problem. I told the crying boy to go get in my car. The foster mom yelled,

"You can't take him! I'm calling the police!"

I said, "I'll do you one better. I'll call the police for you."

The officers came. CPS came. That young woman lost her license that day. And that boy? He's another one of my sons now—grown, healthy, healing, and whole.

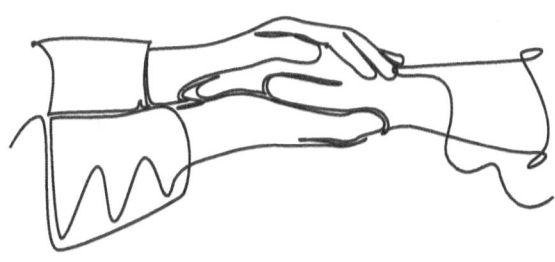

WHEN YOU DON'T MAKE YOUR CHILDREN A PRIORITY — SOMEONE ELSE WILL

THERE'S A TRUTH I'VE LEARNED AS A FOSTER MOTHER, MENTOR, AND WOMAN WHO'S LIVED THROUGH A LOT:

If we don't make our children a priority, someone else will.

And when the wrong people step in, the damage they do can last a lifetime.

I want to speak to the mothers right now—the ones still carrying silent pain. Maybe it's addiction. Maybe you've been in survival mode so long you forgot what peace feels like. Maybe you were hurt so deeply you didn't think you could raise your kids the way they deserved.

I NEED YOU TO KNOW:

This world is not kind to children who aren't protected.

REFLECTION
Healing After the Story

* What about your child(ren) frustrates or angers you the most?

* What part of your own upbringing might be contributing to those triggers?

* Write a letter to the child version of yourself. What does she need to hear?

THERE'S A TRUTH I'VE LEARNED AS A FOSTER MOTHER...
Don't Make Choices Your Children Pay For

TO EVERY WOMAN READING THIS:

Please don't let your personal pain become your child's reality.

Don't let loneliness, addiction, or heartbreak be the reason your kids grow up unprotected.

It is not just about giving birth. It's about showing up. Every day.

I've fostered and raised boys for over two decades, and I can tell you—every child remembers who protected them. Every child remembers who made them feel safe. And every child will eventually realize who didn't.

Let that realization be a source of healing—not heartbreak.

AFFIRMATIONS
"Renewing My Mind"

I am not what I feel—I am what God says.

My thoughts do not control me. I control my thoughts.

I release what no longer serves me—mentally, emotionally, and spiritually.

Peace is not a luxury. It's my birthright.

Interactive Journal

WHO DID YOU CHOOSE OVER YOUR CHILD AND WHY?

Reflection Prompt

Reflect on a time when your priorities may have placed someone or something before your child. Why did it happen, and how do you feel about it now?

_____

_____

_____

_____

_____

_____

_____

SELF-CHECK

Circle which ones apply to you most often:

☐ I have put a relationship before my child's needs.

☐ I have chosen work or ambition over time with my child.

☐ I have allowed fear of being alone to influence my parenting choices.

☐ I have overlooked my child's feelings to please someone else.

☐ I have struggled with guilt over choices I've made.

AFFIRMATION
Prayer Space

AFFIRMATION TO WRITE & REPEAT:

"I will not let past choices define me. Each day is a chance to prioritize love, healing, and my child's well-being."

REWRITE IT SEVERAL TIMES BELOW:

_____

_____

_____

_____

_____

_____

_____

_____

ACTION STEP

What is one intentional step you can take today to rebuild trust and show your child they are your priority?

_____

_____

_____

_____

GIVE YOUR PARENTS A PASS
Last Thought

As we get older, it becomes easier to look back and point out what our parents should've done differently.

Maybe they weren't as emotionally available as we needed.

Maybe they missed some of the signs of our pain.

Maybe they said things or made decisions we still carry with us today.

But here's what I've come to understand...

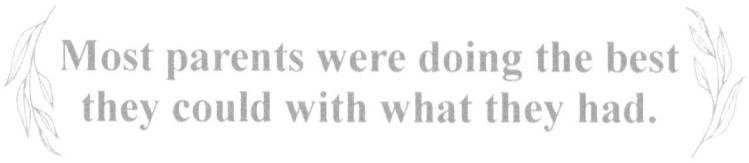

> **Most parents were doing the best they could with what they had.**

My parents are 80 and 79 years old now. And I've had to stop myself many times from judging them by today's standards or my current level of awareness.

The truth is—they had their own storms to weather, their own burdens to carry. Life wasn't easy for them, and they were learning as they went.

The fact that I'm still here—growing, learning, thriving—is proof that they did *something* right.

No, they weren't perfect. But guess what? Neither am I.

THE BIBLE SAYS,

"Honor your father and mother so that your days may be long."

And I truly believe that.

Not because they earned perfection—but because they gave me life, protection, and values I still carry to this day.

I pray that I can be half the parent my mother and father were to me and my brothers.

I pray that I extend to them the same grace I hope my own children will extend to me.

Give your parents a pass—not because they never failed,
but because they kept going.

Forgive them.

Love them.

And most importantly, thank them.

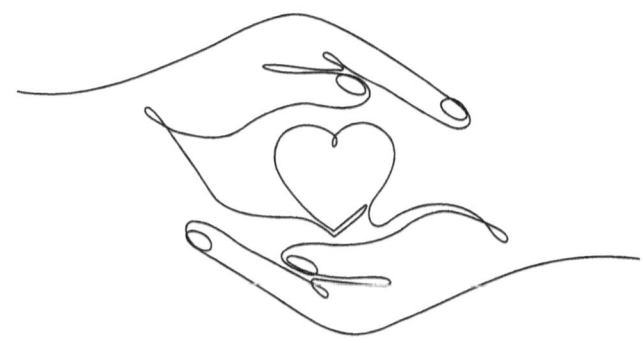

Interactive Journal

20 BIBLE VERSES OF ENCOURAGEMENT

Marriage & Relationships Reflection

EPHESIANS 5:25 – "Husbands, love your wives, just as Christ loved the church and gave himself up for her."

HEBREWS 13:4 – "Marriage should be honored by all, and the marriage bed kept pure, for God will judge the adulterer and all the sexually immoral."

Reflection: How can you honor God in your marriage or relationships?

_____

_____

_____

_____

_____

_____

_____

_____

_____

_____

_____

_____

_____

_____

_____

_____

Mental Health, Anxiety, Depression

2 TIMOTHY 1:7 – "For the Spirit God gave us does not make us timid, but gives us power, love and self-discipline."

PSALM 34:17-18 – "The righteous cry out, and the Lord hears them; he delivers them from all their troubles. The Lord is close to the brokenhearted and saves those who are crushed in spirit."

PHILIPPIANS 4:6-7 – "Do not be anxious about anything, but in every situation, by prayer and petition, with thanksgiving, present your requests to God. And the peace of God, which transcends all understanding, will guard your hearts and your minds in Christ Jesus."

Reflection: What anxious thoughts do you need to surrender to God today?

Love

1 Corinthians 13:4-5 – "Love is patient, love is kind. It does not envy, it does not boast, it is not proud. It does not dishonor others, it is not self-seeking, it is not easily angered, it keeps no record of wrongs."

1 Peter 4:8 – "Above all, love each other deeply, because love covers over a multitude of sins."

John 15:12 – "My command is this: Love each other as I have loved you."

Reflection: How can you show Christlike love to someone this week?

Child Protection / Abuse

Matthew 18:6 – "If anyone causes one of these little ones—those who believe in me—to stumble, it would be better for them to have a large millstone hung around their neck and to be drowned in the depths of the sea."

Proverbs 22:6 – "Start children off on the way they should go, and even when they are old they will not turn from it."

Reflection: How can you be a voice of protection and encouragement for children around you?

Forgiveness

COLOSSIANS 3:13 – "Bear with each other and forgive one another if any of you has a grievance against someone. Forgive as the Lord forgave you."

MATTHEW 6:14-15 – "For if you forgive other people when they sin against you, your heavenly Father will also forgive you. But if you do not forgive others their sins, your Father will not forgive your sins."

EPHESIANS 4:32 – "Be kind and compassionate to one another, forgiving each other, just as in Christ God forgave you."

Reflection: Who do you need to release through forgiveness today?

Overcoming the Enemy

1 PETER 5:8-9 – "Be alert and of sober mind. Your enemy the devil prowls around like a roaring lion looking for someone to devour. Resist him, standing firm in the faith…"

JAMES 4:7 – "Submit yourselves, then, to God. Resist the devil, and he will flee from you."

JOHN 10:10 – "The thief comes only to steal and kill and destroy; I have come that they may have life, and have it to the full."

Reflection: In what areas of your life do you need to resist the enemy's traps?

Hope & Renewal

ISAIAH 41:10 – "So do not fear, for I am with you; do not be dismayed, for I am your God. I will strengthen you and help you; I will uphold you with my righteous right hand."

ROMANS 8:28 – "And we know that in all things God works for the good of those who love him, who have been called according to his purpose."

JEREMIAH 29:11 – "For I know the plans I have for you," declares the Lord, "plans to prosper you and not to harm you, plans to give you hope and a future."

PSALM 30:5 – "Weeping may stay for the night, but rejoicing comes in the morning."

Reflection: Which of these promises brings you the most comfort today?

RECYCLE BIN
Who to Keep in Your Life and Who to Remove

Reflection Prompt

Think about the people in your life. Who pours into you and helps you grow, and who drains your energy or holds you back? List them below.

Keep (People who build me up):

_____

_____

_____

_____

Remove (People who drain or harm me):

_____

_____

_____

_____

SELF-CHECK

Circle which ones you've experienced:

- ☐ I struggle to let go of toxic relationships.
- ☐ I keep people in my life out of guilt or fear of being alone.
- ☐ I feel energized after being with certain people.
- ☐ I notice my values don't align with everyone I spend time with.
- ☐ I often give second chances without boundaries.

AFFIRMATION
Prayer Space

AFFIRMATION TO WRITE & REPEAT:

"I have the courage to release what harms me and the wisdom to keep what grows me."

REWRITE IT SEVERAL TIMES BELOW:

_____

_____

_____

_____

_____

_____

_____

_____

_____

ACTION STEP

What is one healthy boundary you will set this week with someone in your life?

_____

_____

_____

_____

_____

THERE ARE SO MANY AMAZING THINGS ABOUT YOU
Let's Write Them Down

Reflection Prompt

Take a moment to list the qualities, strengths, and blessings that make you unique and amazing. Don't hold back—write down as many as you can think of!

_____

_____

_____

_____

_____

_____

_____

SELF-CHECK

Circle which affirmations you believe are true about yourself (even if you struggle to say them):

☐ I am resilient.

☐ I am worthy of love.

☐ I bring joy to others.

☐ I have overcome challenges with strength.

☐ I am creative and gifted.

☐ I make a difference in the lives of others.

AFFIRMATION
Prayer Space

AFFIRMATION TO WRITE & REPEAT:

"I am wonderfully made, and there
are amazing things about me
worth celebrating."

REWRITE IT SEVERAL TIMES BELOW:

_____

_____

_____

_____

_____

_____

_____

_____

_____

ACTION STEP

Choose three amazing qualities you listed. How will you intentionally
live them out this week?

_____

_____

_____

_____

WHEN AM I THE PROBLEM?

Reflection Prompt

Think of a time when you realized you might have contributed to a problem. What role did you play, and what did you learn from it?

_____

_____

_____

_____

_____

_____

_____

_____

_____

_____

_____

_____

SELF-CHECK

Circle which ones apply to you most often:

- ☐ I avoid taking responsibility when things go wrong.
- ☐ I blame others before examining my own actions.
- ☐ I notice repeated patterns in my relationships or work.
- ☐ I struggle to admit when I'm wrong.
- ☐ I resist feedback or correction from others.

AFFIRMATION
Prayer Space

AFFIRMATION TO WRITE & REPEAT:

"Acknowledging my flaws is not weakness—it is the first step toward growth and healing."

REWRITE IT SEVERAL TIMES BELOW:

_____

_____

_____

_____

_____

_____

_____

_____

ACTION STEP

What is one area of your life where you can take more responsibility and begin to change?

_____

_____

_____

_____

DEDICATION

To every person silently fighting a war in their mind— this book is for you.

To the strong ones who kept showing up when quitting felt easier.

To the ones who kept smiling when no one saw the tears.

You are not alone. You are not invisible. And you are not what the lies told you.

To the 16 boys my husband and I have raised—thank you for being my greatest teachers in strength, grace, and unconditional love. You've shown me what perseverance, resilience, and purpose look like in real life. Anytime a child is removed from the only family and life they've ever known – placed with stranger after stranger – speaks volumes about the resilience required to survive. You, my sweet children, have already overcome one of life's greatest challenges.

To my husband, Minister John Wilkerson—thank you. For loving me loudly and gently. For celebrating my wins and praying through my losses. For kissing me on my forehead every single night without fail. For protecting my heart, loving my children as your own, and reminding me every day that I am worthy of peace, purpose, and rest. Thank you for encouraging me to go back to school—and pushing me to finish. I'm a better woman because I get to walk this life with you.

To My Chosen Family We may not be connected by blood, but we are forever bound by love. Love you all!! Stella Williams (RIP), Jeanette Walker, Jenee, Jesse, Morgan, Dezmond, Ashley, and Jamar.

To my firstborns, Shane and Antoneisha —thank you for sharing me with so many others. Before I fostered or adopted anyone, it was just us. Your patience, love, and quiet strength have been the steady foundation behind my passion and purpose. You both are the reason I never had the time—or luxury—to fully fall apart, even when I felt like I was breaking. (Smile.) You were my "why" before I ever knew the power of purpose. Because of you, I went back to school and earned not one, but two master's degrees. I chose my circles more carefully. I avoided the traps of addiction, stayed clear of anything illegal, and made decisions rooted in integrity—because I refused to make choices you would one day have to pay for. That says everything about the love I carry for you both. You've given me more motivation than you'll ever understand—and for that, I will always honor you.

To my maternal grandmother, Dorothy Dainty—You are the reason I am balanced. Your wisdom, gentleness, and presence shaped the woman I am. Rest in peace, Queen. Your legacy lives in me. RIP

To my paternal grandmother, Florence Ella Cotton – Your spirit and quiet strength taught me to lead with love and grace. Thank you for showing me that calmness speaks louder than noise. Your legacy lives in me. RIP

To my brothers, Randy and Sean, who stood as my first bodyguards in life – protecting me, guiding me, and showing me what it means to be loved and safe.

And to my very first role models—my parents, Joan Phillips and Ronald Shelby: Thank you for shaping the foundation of who I am. For pouring into me when I didn't yet know my worth. For believing in me when all I had were big dreams and a tender heart. For protecting me, correcting me, and investing in my future before I even understood the value of it. Thank you for listening—really listening—to my hopes, my wild ideas, my voice. For teaching me that the world sees color, but God does not. That kindness is never wasted. That character always matters. And most of all, thank you for introducing me to Jesus when I was still small enough to climb into your lap—because that single gift has carried me through every storm since.

Your love planted the seeds of my purpose. This book is fruit from that soil.

With all my heart,
Kelly

Prayer to
Reset My Mind

God,

Sometimes my thoughts are too loud.

They echo with fear, shame, insecurity, and doubt—

*and before I know it, I'm believing lies I thought
I'd already healed from.*

But I'm tired of living in that headspace.

*Tired of overthinking, overanalyzing, and
overwhelming myself*

with every "what if," every failure, every fear.

So today, I'm giving You access to my thoughts.

*Not just the clean ones—but the dark,
hidden, scary ones too.*

*The ones I don't say out loud. The ones
I pretend don't exist.*

*You already know them. And still,
You call me beautiful.*

God, reset my mind.

Rewire the places that believe pain over promise.

Silence the inner critic that keeps me stuck.

Replace anxiety with peace.
Replace insecurity with boldness.

Remind me that I am not too broken,
too late, or too much.

Help me speak to myself the way
You speak to me—

with grace, with love, with truth, and with power.

I cast down every thought that doesn't
align with Your Word.

And I declare today—my mind is under
new management.

In Jesus' name,

Amen.

THE
UGLY
TRUTH

When Our Thoughts Become Our Worst Enemy

ISBN: 979-8-9999642-0-5

Publisher: Born Behind the 8-Ball, LLC

Printed in the United States of America

Scripture quotations are from the Holy Bible, [(NIV)]

Cover design by Kelly Nichole Wilkerson

Author website: www.KidsBornBehindthe8-Ball.com

www.ingramcontent.com/pod-product-compliance
Lightning Source LLC
Chambersburg PA
CBHW031227120626
46545CB00003B/1020